DK SUPER Planet

MOUNTAINS

Traverse the vast ranges and peaks that shape our planet—from towering fold mountains, to deep underwater mountains in the ocean

Produced for DK by
Editorial Just Content Limited
Design Studio Noel

Author Steve Tomecek

Senior Editor Amelia Jones
Senior Art Editor Gilda Pacitti
Managing Editor Katherine Neep
Managing Art Editor Sarah Corcoran
Production Editor Jaypal Chauhan
DTP Designer Rohit Singh
Production Controller Rebecca Parton
Publisher Sarah Forbes
Managing Director, Learning Hilary Fine

First American Edition, 2025
Published in the United States by DK Publishing,
a division of Penguin Random House LLC
1745 Broadway, 20th Floor, New York, NY 10019

Copyright © 2025 Dorling Kindersley Limited
25 26 27 28 29 10 9 8 7 6 5 4 3 2 1
001–345526–Apr/2025

All rights reserved.
Without limiting the rights under the copyright reserved above, no part of this publication may be reproduced, stored in or introduced into a retrieval system, or transmitted, in any form, or by any means (electronic, mechanical, photocopying, recording, or otherwise), without the prior written permission of the copyright owner.
Published in Great Britain by Dorling Kindersley Limited

A catalog record for this book
is available from the Library of Congress.
HC ISBN: 978-0-5939-6606-8
PB ISBN: 978-0-5939-6605-1

DK books are available at special discounts when purchased in bulk for sales promotions, premiums, fund-raising, or educational use.
For details, contact: DK Publishing Special Markets,
1745 Broadway, 20th Floor, New York, NY 10019
SpecialSales@dk.com

Printed and bound in China

www.dk.com

This book was made with Forest Stewardship Council™ certified paper – one small step in DK's commitment to a sustainable future. Learn more at www.dk.com/uk/information/sustainability

Contents

What is a Mountain?	4
Plate Tectonics	6
Types of Mountains	8
Fold Mountains	10
Case Study: The Himalayas	12
Life in the Himalayas	14
Fault-Block Mountains	16
Case Study: The Sierra Nevada	18
Life in the Sierra Nevada	20
Volcanic Mountains	22
Case Study: Mount Kilimanjaro	24
Life on Mount Kilimanjaro	26
Erosional Mountains	28
Case Study: Uluru	30
Underwater Mountains	32
Everyday Science: Monitoring Volcanoes	34
Everyday Science: Mountain Glaciers and Climate Change	36
Let's Experiment! Make a Fossil	38
Let's Experiment! Make a Model Volcano	40
Vocabulary Builder: The Life and Death of a Mountain	42
Glossary	44
Index	46

Words in **bold** are explained in the glossary on page 44.

What is a MOUNTAIN?

Mountains are amazing. A mountain is a landform that rises high above the surrounding area. No two look alike. They are all over Earth, including in the ocean. They stretch high into the sky, giving stunning views of the world below. Some stand alone, dominating the landscape. Most are in **mountain ranges**.

Mountains affect the weather and climate near them. They are also **ecosystems** that are home to many different animals and plants.

Each continent has mountain ranges. The longest is the Andes, at about 5,500 miles (8,900 km). The Andes Mountains are in South America.

Fascinating fact

People have identified more than 1 million mountains on Earth.

Mountains have been important to many **civilizations**. They are natural barriers that prevent people and animals from easily moving from one area to another.

In general, a landform that rises high above Earth's surface is a mountain. All mountains have some features in common.

RIDGE
A ridge is a long, thin strip of raised land across a mountain.

SUMMIT
A summit is the highest point on a mountain that can be measured.

SLOPE
A slope is the side of a mountain that rises from the base.

PEAK
A peak is a pointed area at or near the top of a mountain.

VALLEY
A valley is a low area between two mountain peaks or ridges.

BASE
A base is the point where a mountain rises from the surrounding surface.

Plate TECTONICS

Have you ever noticed that some of the continents seem like they could fit together, like pieces of a giant jigsaw? Scientists believe that long ago, all the continents were joined together in one landmass. Over time, the landmass changed and broke apart into continents. They moved to their current position over millions of years. Today, we can explain this using **plate tectonics**.

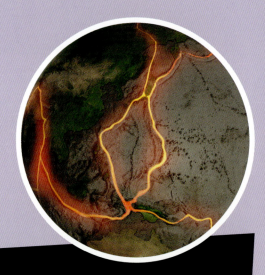

Earth is made up of different layers. Huge slabs of rock float on Earth's **crust**, on top of the **mantle**. These slabs are **tectonic plates**.

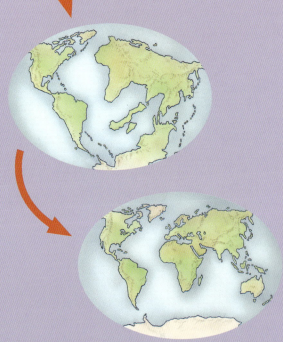

Fascinating fact

Different tectonic plates move at different rates. But they all move slowly. The average speed is about 0.6 in (1.5 cm) per year.

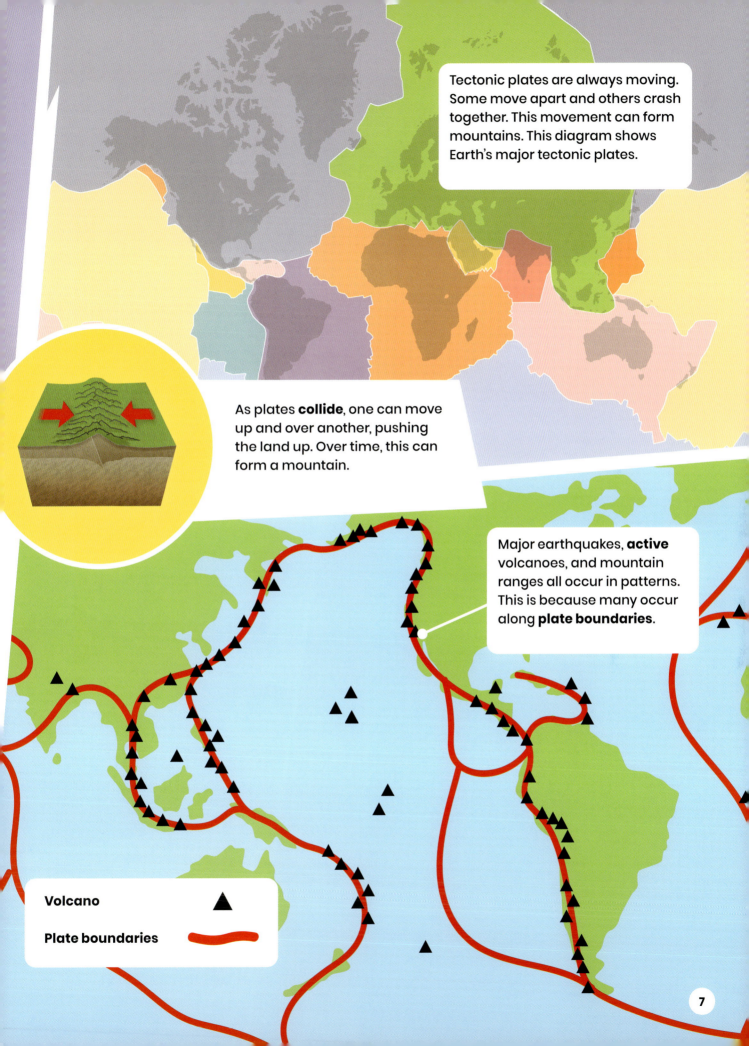

Tectonic plates are always moving. Some move apart and others crash together. This movement can form mountains. This diagram shows Earth's major tectonic plates.

As plates **collide**, one can move up and over another, pushing the land up. Over time, this can form a mountain.

Major earthquakes, **active** volcanoes, and mountain ranges all occur in patterns. This is because many occur along **plate boundaries**.

Volcano ▲

Plate boundaries ━━

Types of MOUNTAINS

There are more than a million different mountains on Earth. Each one is unique in its location and appearance. One reason for this is that mountains can form in several ways. Here are four of the most common types of mountains.

FAULT-BLOCK MOUNTAIN
When tectonic plates pull apart or slide past each other, this can create **faults**. Some rock rises, creating steep mountains. Steens Mountain in Oregon is an example of this.

FOLD MOUNTAIN
When tectonic plates collide, rocks between them get pushed higher and higher. This can form a fold mountain. Mount Elbert in the Rocky Mountains, USA, is a fold mountain.

VOLCANIC MOUNTAIN
When **magma** erupts from a volcano, new layers of rock build up. Over time, this forms a volcanic mountain, such as Mount Fuji in Japan.

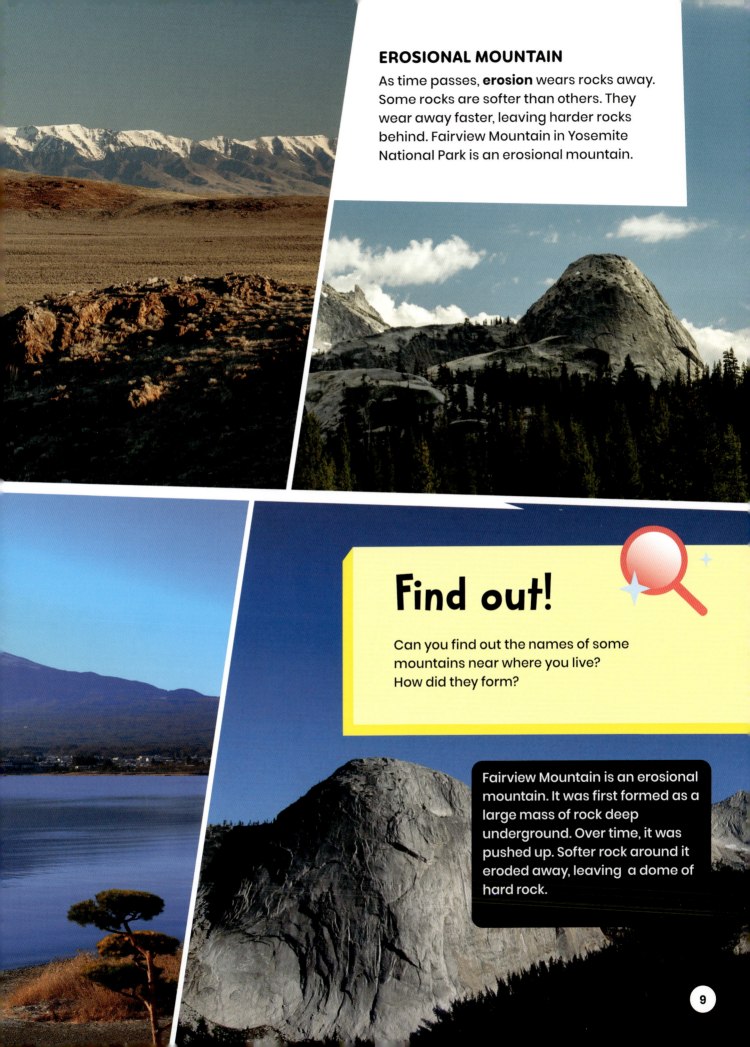

EROSIONAL MOUNTAIN

As time passes, **erosion** wears rocks away. Some rocks are softer than others. They wear away faster, leaving harder rocks behind. Fairview Mountain in Yosemite National Park is an erosional mountain.

Find out!

Can you find out the names of some mountains near where you live? How did they form?

Fairview Mountain is an erosional mountain. It was first formed as a large mass of rock deep underground. Over time, it was pushed up. Softer rock around it eroded away, leaving a dome of hard rock.

Fold MOUNTAINS

The Alps, Andes, and Himalayas are some of the most impressive mountain ranges on Earth. They are also all fold mountains. Fold mountains often start as flat layers of rock. These layers get trapped between two tectonic plates that move toward each other. As the plates collide, the rock layers get pushed higher and higher. This forms a mountain.

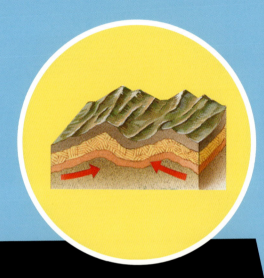

Fold mountains take millions of years to form. They appear along current and ancient plate boundaries, where two continental landforms crashed together.

Fascinating fact

The Appalachian Mountains in North America first formed about 300 million years ago. **Geologists** believe that when the Appalachians were young, they were as high as the Andes are now.

Once the tectonic plates stop colliding, the mountains start to erode. This takes hundreds of millions of years.

Geologists study older fold mountains to try to find out how tectonic plates moved in the past. This helps them understand Earth's history.

When rocks undergo slow, steady pressure for a very long time, they can form structures called folds.

This image was taken from space. You can see the folded structure of the Appalachian Mountains in the eastern USA.

Case Study: THE HIMALAYAS

The Himalayas are one of the world's most awesome mountain ranges. While the Andes form the longest continental mountain chain in the world, the Himalayas are the highest. Geologists believe these fold mountains started forming about 55 million years ago, when two tectonic plates collided.

The Himalayas make a large, curving band through central Asia. Ice and snow cover the mountaintops. This is the source of water for many rivers.

Because the Himalayas rise so high, the weather can be harsh. Some animals and plants have special **adaptations** to survive the difficult conditions.

Fascinating fact

The 10 highest mountains in the world are in the Himalayas.

Red pandas live in forests at lower **elevations** of the Himalayas. Due to **habitat** destruction, fewer than 10,000 remain in the wild.

Snow leopards have thick gray fur. Their wide, furry paws make walking on snow easy. Strong legs help them jump between rock ledges.

The Himalayan tahr lives on mountain slopes. It sheds its thick fur coat in the summer. Its hooves grip well on steep rock faces.

The deodar cedar grows between 5,000–10,000 ft (1,500–3,200 m) above sea level. Its shallow roots hold soil in place on steep mountain slopes.

Life in the HIMALAYAS

The Himalayan **environment** can be harsh. But the people who call these mountains home have adapted to their conditions. Scientists are not sure when people began settling in the Himalayas. An analysis of some footprints preserved in rock suggests that it could be as long as 12,000 years ago. Today, more than 50 million people live in the Himalayas.

Kibber Village is located at 14,010 ft (4,270 m) above sea level. It is the highest village in the world.

Kathmandu is the largest city in the Himalayas. More than 850,000 people live there. Most of the Himalayan population live in smaller towns and villages.

Fascinating fact

Some Himalayan people burn dried yak dung as fuel. They live high up in the mountains where there are no trees or grasses to burn.

Many Himalayan people are farmers. They grow buckwheat, rice, barley, and millet. Millet can be served like rice or turned into flour and used in baking.

Broom grass grows wild in the Himalayas, but farmers also grow it. It can be used as animal food, burned as fuel, and made into brooms.

The Himalayas span a huge area. They are home to people who have many cultures and speak lots of different languages.

Yaks are important livestock in the Himalayas. They pull and carry heavy loads. They also provide milk, meat, and wool for clothes.

Fault-Block MOUNTAINS

Like fold mountains, fault-block mountains also form due to plate tectonics. But they do not form due to plates pushing up and over each other. Instead, they form along faults or cracks in Earth's surface. Here, huge chunks of rock slide past or move away from each other, forming mountains.

The Teton Range in Wyoming, USA, are fault-block mountains. They formed over millions of years and are part of the Rocky Mountains.

Fascinating fact

The Basin and Range Province extends across the western USA and into Mexico. It contains hundreds of fault-block mountains. Some are still in the process of forming.

Fault-block mountains do not get as long or high as fold mountains. They tend to form inland rather than along plate boundaries.

When tectonic plates slide or move apart, large chunks of rock slide down. This leaves steep-sided blocks that stick up to form mountains.

Most fault-block mountains have at least one steep side and a gently sloping side. Since they form near cracks in Earth's surface, they are also often near deep valleys.

The Harz Mountains in Germany are fault-block mountains. The range is 68 miles (110 km) long and 22 miles (35 km) wide. This mountain range is surrounded by many long and narrow valleys.

Case Study: THE SIERRA NEVADA

The Sierra Nevada mountains are in California, in the western USA. This fault-block mountain range stretches 400 miles (640 km) and is up to 80 miles (129 km) wide in some places. There are hundreds of mountain peaks in the Sierra Nevada. The mountain range is home to three national parks and 10 national forests.

Mount Whitney is the highest mountain in the Sierra Nevada. It is also the highest mountain in the continental USA.

Find out!

The Sierra Nevada is home to huge trees called giant sequoias. Can you find out how long they can live?

Over 3,000 years.

Sierra fence lizards blend in well with their surroundings as they are camouflaged when they sit on rocks and trees. Their main diet is spiders, crickets, ticks, and scorpions.

Giant sequoias only grow on the western slopes of the Sierra Nevada. They can grow to over 300 ft (94 m) and weigh over 6,000 tons (5,400 metric tons).

The great gray owls of the Sierra Nevada are **endangered**. There are only around 300 left in California.

Tahoe yellow cress only grows on the shores of Lake Tahoe. People are trying to protect this rare plant's habitat.

Sierra bighorn sheep jump easily between rocky mountain slopes. They eat grasses and other vegetation.

Life in
THE SIERRA NEVADA

People have lived in the Sierra Nevada for thousands of years. **Indigenous** American settlements in the area date back to around 1,500 years ago. In the 1800s, gold was discovered in California. This brought hundreds of thousands of people to the Sierra Nevada in search of fortune. Today, the region is home to many towns and cities.

Many people live around Lake Tahoe, with over 20,000 in the town of South Lake Tahoe. The lake is a popular tourist destination.

Lake Tahoe is known for its winter sports, including skiing and snowboarding. Ski resorts are important to the region's **economy**.

Nevada City, California, was first settled during the gold rush. It is a typical mountain town in the Sierra Nevada.

El Capitan is a towering block of granite in Yosemite National Park. It is popular with rock climbers.

People come from all over the world to visit General Sherman, a 2,300-year-old giant sequoia, in Kings Canyon National Park.

Fascinating fact

Over 3 million people visit Yosemite National Park each year.

Sequoia National Park was established in 1890 to protect giant sequoias from **logging**. It was the second national park created in the USA.

Volcanic MOUNTAINS

A volcano is an opening in Earth's crust that erupts magma and hot **ash**. When layers of ash or cooled magma build up, this can form volcanic mountains. Volcanic mountains can look quite different depending on what they are made of. There are volcanic mountains all over the world. Most are on plate boundaries.

Mount Hood in Oregon, USA, is a **composite volcano**, which is the tallest kind. This means it is made up of cooled **lava** and ash that have built up into a tall cone.

Mount Hood is part of the Cascade Range, which extends from Canada to Northern California. It contains 18 volcanoes, most of which are active.

Fascinating fact

There are around 1,350 active volcanoes on Earth.

Parícutin in Mexico is a **cinder cone** volcano. Its sandy sides make it a challenging hike. Cinder cones are the smallest type of volcano.

As a volcano erupts, the lava or ash builds up in layers around the volcano's opening. Over time, this can form a volcanic mountain.

Shield volcanoes are larger and wider than composite volcanoes. Piton de la Fournaise is a shield volcano on Réunion Island in the Indian Ocean.

Case Study: MOUNT KILIMANJARO

Mount Kilimanjaro is the highest point in Africa. It is the largest freestanding mountain on Earth. It is formed of three volcanoes called Mawensi, Shira, and Kibo. Mawensi and Shira are **extinct**, so they are very unlikely to erupt again. But Kibo is **dormant**—it could erupt in the future.

Plate tectonics helped form Mount Kilimanjaro. It is near the East African Rift Valley, where the African continent is splitting apart.

Even though it is near the equator, snow usually covers Mount Kilimanjaro's peak. This is because it is so high.

As the plates moved apart, Earth's crust thinned. Magma rose from below Earth's surface and formed dozens of volcanoes, including Mount Kilimanjaro.

Fascinating fact

The **glaciers** on Mount Kilimanjaro are melting due to climate change. Many scientists fear they will disappear by 2050.

Mount Kilimanjaro hosts many ecosystems, from farms to **moorland**, **rainforest**, and **tundra**.

Serval cats live in the upper moorlands of Mount Kilimanjaro. They hunt alone, eating smaller animals.

Abbott's duiker antelopes live in the mountain's high forested areas. They are endangered.

Giant lobelias are flowering plants, native to the mountains of Tanzania. They grow in the moorlands of Mount Kilimanjaro.

Jackson's chameleons camouflage themselves in the mountain's forests. Their eyes move independently to look for predators.

Life on MOUNT KILIMANJARO

Mount Kilimanjaro is the home of the Indigenous Chagga people. Their **ancestors** came to the region in the 11th century CE. These early settlers found the foothills of the mountain perfect for growing crops like bananas, maize, and yams. Mount Kilimanjaro is a popular destination for tourists and hikers. Each year, around 30,000 try to reach the summit.

In 1973, Kilimanjaro National Park was set up to protect the mountain and six surrounding forests. It is also a UNESCO World Heritage site.

Fascinating fact

There are many theories for what "Kilimanjaro" means, including "White Mountain" and "Shining Mountain." Some Chagga tribes call it by a name that means "Mountain Where Birds Cannot Fly."

The Chagga's traditional grass huts have a cone shape. People often grew pineapples around the house to keep snakes away.

Today, the Chagga people live in modern homes. Many still farm the land. Bananas and coffee are the main crops in the area.

People buy and sell fresh fruit, vegetables, and other goods at village markets.

The Chagga people have lived in Marangu village on the slopes of Mount Kilimanjaro since the 1800s. It is a popular place to start the hike up the mountain.

Erosional MOUNTAINS

Most mountains form due to the movement of tectonic plates or the eruptions of volcanoes. But some mountains form as a result of erosion. These mountains are found all over the world. As soft rock erodes or wears away, it leaves harder rock behind. This hard rock forms an erosional mountain. **Weathering** and erosion work together to form erosional mountains. Weathering breaks down rocks into smaller pieces, and then erosion carries them away. The pieces can be carried by wind, water, or ice.

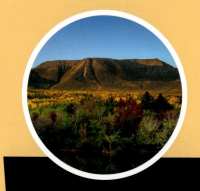

Mount Katahdin is the highest mountain in Maine, USA. It is an erosional mountain.

Kirkjufell Mountain is in Iceland. Erosion from glaciers formed its distinctive shape.

These diagrams show four common causes of weathering and erosion: water, ice, temperature changes, and living things, such as plant roots.

As water gets into cracks in rock, it can freeze and cause the rock to break apart.

Rainfall can wear away rock.

Changes in temperature can cause rock to crack and erode.

Plant roots can break rock apart as they grow.

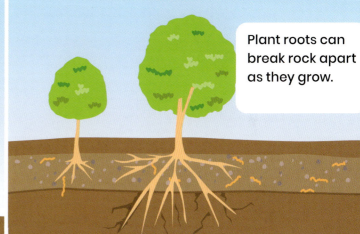

Fascinating fact

Even though the granite of Mount Rushmore is very hard, erosion still occurs. Workers fill small cracks in the sculpture with special cement to keep the presidents' faces intact.

Before presidents' heads were carved into it, Mount Rushmore in South Dakota, USA, was formed by erosion.

Case Study: ULURU

Uluru is one of the most recognizable erosional landforms in the world. It is a massive chunk of red sandstone. Its summit is 2,831 ft (863 m) above sea level, making it the highest point for miles around. Uluru is in a national park in central Australia. Thousands of tourists visit each year.

Uluru is formed from a hard sandstone, which is a type of soft rock. Over time, the sandstone eroded, leaving Uluru as we know it now.

Many scientists regard Uluru as a monolith, not a mountain. This is because it is a single block of rock.

Fascinating fact

Most of Uluru is below ground level. You would need to dig down another 3.5 miles (6 km) to reach the bottom of it.

Over time, erosion has created many caves along Uluru's base. **Aboriginal peoples** have used these caves as living sites and for rituals.

Uluru is very important to Aboriginal peoples. People are not allowed to climb Uluru as it is a sacred place.

Many plants flourish in the dry desert environment around Uluru. These include mulga and eucalyptus trees.

Some of the animals found in the park include geckos, skinks, and snakes. There are also around 175 different types of birds.

Red kangaroos are a common sight in the area surrounding Uluru.

Underwater MOUNTAINS

Scientists used to think the deep ocean floor was flat. By the late 1800s, research showed mountains and valleys in the seafloor. Then, in 1977, two scientists used **sonar** to make a map of the ocean floor. The map showed a long chain of underwater mountains that circle Earth. This was the mid-ocean ridge.

Fascinating fact

The tallest mountain on Earth is Mauna Kea on the island of Hawai'i, in the USA. When measured from the seafloor, Mauna Kea is almost 34,000 ft (10,211 m) tall.

The mid-ocean ridge is the longest mountain range on Earth. It wraps nearly 40,390 miles (65,000 km) around the planet.

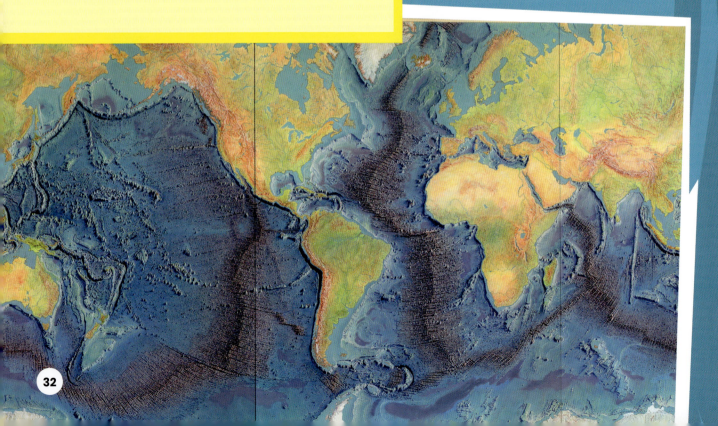

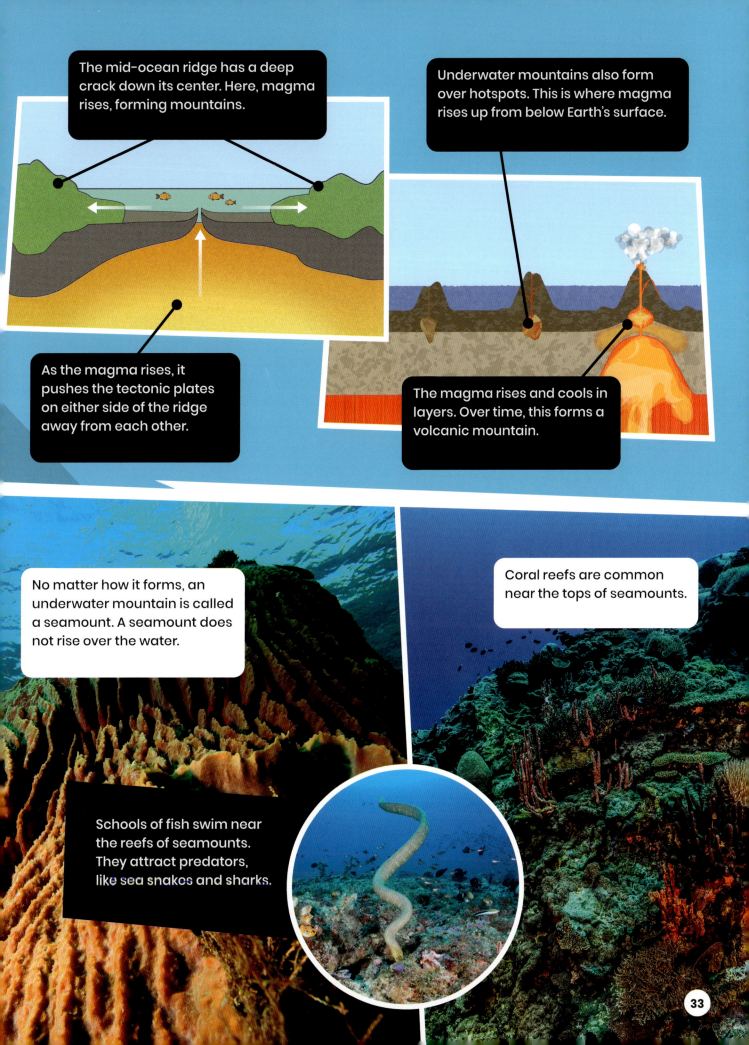

Everyday SCIENCE
Monitoring Volcanoes

Geologists study mountains to learn how they form. In some places on Earth, they can observe plate tectonics in action. But these processes work slowly. It takes years to see changes. When a volcano erupts, you can see its effects right away. At the Hawaiian Volcano Observatory (HVO), scientists observe and monitor the Kīlauea volcano.

The Hawaiian volcanoes are shield volcanoes. Their eruptions are more predictable and less explosive than other volcanoes.

Scientists at HVO test lava samples from Kīlauea. Lava temperatures can reach 2,200°F (1,200°C). Even when it has cooled, it is dangerous to get close.

For years, HVO was located on the rim of the volcano. In 2018, earthquakes and eruptions damaged the building. It was moved to a safer site.

Everyday SCIENCE
Mountain Glaciers and Climate Change

Due to climate change, heat waves, droughts, and extreme weather events are increasing worldwide. One of the biggest problems is on top of some of the world's highest mountains. A lot of the mountain glaciers on these high peaks are melting. And this could have severe consequences for many people on Earth.

Glaciers form near mountain summits, where temperatures are rarely above freezing. These huge rivers of ice flow downhill.

Glaciers are made of fresh water. Scientists estimate that almost 2 billion people depend on glacier **meltwater** for drinking.

Meltwater also flows into streams that feed larger rivers. Meltwater from the Himalayas feeds big rivers like the Ganges, Yangtze, Huáng Hé, and Brahmaputra.

Before, 2009

All glaciers grow and melt over time. But now, glaciers are melting at an alarming rate.

After, 2018

The World Glacier Monitoring Service collects data on mountain glaciers. It uses photos, satellite images, and ice measurements to see how fast they melt.

It may be too late for some mountain glaciers. Scientists predict glaciers will melt completely in some places in the next 50 years.

If mountain glaciers vanish, this will harm the billions of people who need meltwater for drinking, energy, and watering crops.

Let's EXPERIMENT!

MAKE A FOSSIL

We often find **fossils** in mountains due to the processes of plate tectonics and erosion. In this experiment, you will make your own fossil.

You will need:
- Plaster of Paris and some water
- A spoon
- A plastic cup
- Modeling clay
- A plastic bowl
- A shell
- Paint
- A paintbrush

Ask an adult to help you mix and pour the plaster of Paris. If you touch it, rinse and then wash your hands with soap and water.

1 Use a spoon to mix the plaster of Paris with water in a plastic cup.

2 Place the modeling clay in the bottom of the bowl and press down. It should be about 0.75 in (2 cm) thick.

3 Press your shell into the modeling clay. Hold it for 30 seconds, then lift it out.

4 Pour the plaster of Paris on top of the modeling clay. Leave it for at least 12 hours to harden.

5 Once the plaster has set, carefully lift it out of the bowl.

6 You can now paint and display your fossil!

Let's EXPERIMENT!

MAKE A MODEL VOLCANO

Some mountains, like Mount Kilimanjaro, are volcanic. In this experiment, you will make your own model volcano.

You will need:
- A small plastic bottle
- Scissors
- Packing tape
- A large piece of cardboard
- Some newspaper
- A bowl
- 14 oz (400 g) of flour
- Water
- A spoon
- Paintbrush
- Some paint

Be careful when using scissors. You can ask an adult to cut the plastic bottle for you.

1 Cut the top section off a plastic bottle. Use packing tape to stick it to the cardboard. Ball up pieces of newspaper. Tape them to the base of the bottle.

2 Mix flour and water to make a paste. Place strips of newspaper in the paste. Add the strips in layers over the bottle and taped newspaper balls.

3 Keep adding newspaper strips until you have a volcano shape. Leave it to dry.

4 When your volcano is dry, paint it. Your model is ready!

MOUNT NGĀURUHOE, NEW ZEALAND

Mount Ngāuruhoe is a volcano in New Zealand. It first erupted around 2,500 years ago. Ngāuruhoe is a Māori word. It means "throwing hot stones." It is a reminder of how this volcanic mountain was formed.

Vocabulary BUILDER

The Life and Death of a Mountain

The Taconic Mountains are in the US state of New York. Long ago, they were as high as the Himalayas. Read the description about how they have changed over millions of years.

The Taconic Mountains first formed more than 400 million years ago. At this time, they were rocks on the edge of a tectonic plate. An ancient sea was located to the east. Slowly, the tectonic plate under the sea moved west. It collided with the plate underneath the Taconic Mountains. This collision pushed them up, transforming them into high fold mountains.

Over time, rain and ice wore the mountains down. They started to weather and break apart. Erosion from wind and water carried huge amounts of **sediment** down mountain streams. It **deposited** the sediment in a sea to the west. The mountains changed a lot in the last 2 million years. During the last **ice age**, huge glaciers flowed over the area. The glaciers ground down and eroded the mountains. As the glaciers moved, they scraped rock off the tops of the mountains. This is what shaped the round peaks that the mountains have today. Now, due to their smaller size, many of the Taconic Mountains are more like hills than mountains.

Things that can shape mountains: collision, erosion, glacier, ice, mountain, peak, rain, rock, sea, sediment, stream, tectonic plate, water, wind

Action words to describe mountains: become, break apart, carry, collide, deposit, flow, grind down, move, push, scrape away, shape, soar, transform, wear down, weather

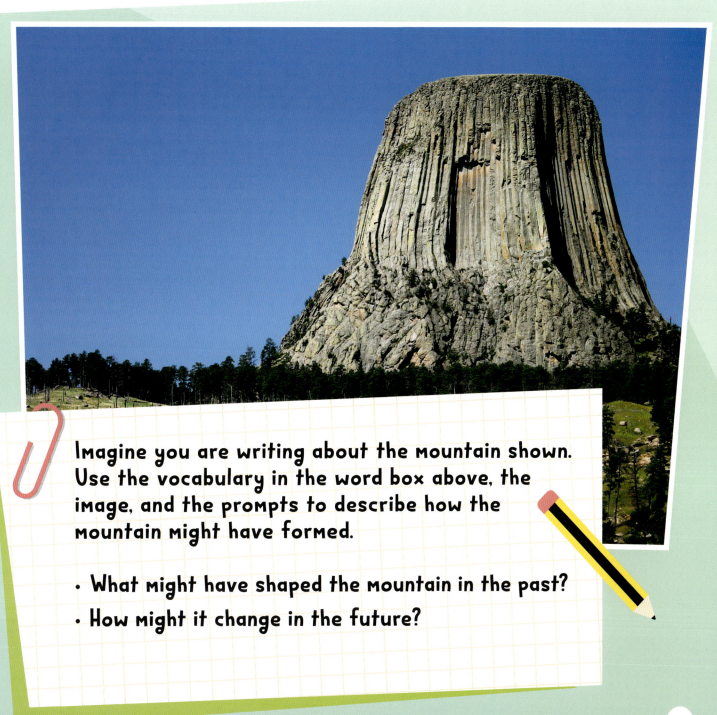

Imagine you are writing about the mountain shown. Use the vocabulary in the word box above, the image, and the prompts to describe how the mountain might have formed.

- What might have shaped the mountain in the past?
- How might it change in the future?

Glossary

Aboriginal peoples The Indigenous peoples of Australia and most of the region's islands.

Active Used to describe a volcano that is still erupting, though many years can pass between eruptions.

Adaptation The process in which a plant or animal changes itself as a result of its environment, either to increase its ability to survive or reproduce.

Ancestor Someone from whom a person is descended.

Ash A mixture of very small pieces of rock, minerals, and glass that comes out of a volcano during an eruption.

Caldera A large, bowl-shaped crater that forms when a volcano erupts and collapses on itself.

Cinder cone A type of volcano that is formed from layers of ash.

Civilization Any human society in the past or present that has culture and technology.

Collide To bump into one another with force.

Composite volcano A type of volcano made up of layers of hardened lava and rock. This is the tallest type of volcano, and is also called a stratovolcano.

Crust Earth's top-most layer, the surface.

Deposit To place or put something down.

Dormant Used to describe a volcano that is not active, but may become active in the future.

Economy The system of making, using, and trading goods in an area, such as a town or country.

Ecosystem A community of living things that interact with non-living things in their environment.

Elevation The height of a landform, such as a mountain, from sea level.

Endangered An animal that is at risk of going extinct.

Environment The place where a plant or animal lives, and the interactions it has with the living and non-living things there.

Erosion A process caused by wind, water, and ice that breaks down and carries material such as rock and sediment from one area to another.

Extinct Used to describe a volcano that is very unlikely to become active in the future.

Fault Cracks in Earth's crust where tectonic plates can move against or pull apart from each other.

Fossil The preserved remains, or trace, of an ancient plant or animal.

Geologist A scientist who studies the history of Earth, its structure, and the processes that shape it.

Glacier A large river of ice that flows slowly over the land.

Habitat An environment where plants, animals, and other organisms live.

Ice age A long period when icy glaciers cover large areas of land.

Indigenous Originating from a specific place, often used in reference to peoples.

Lava Very hot liquid or semiliquid rock found on Earth's surface as a result of a volcanic eruption.

Logging The process of cutting down trees in order to use them to make things, such as paper and wood for building.

Magma Very hot liquid or semiliquid rock found under Earth's surface.

Mantle The largest layer of Earth, lying between the crust and the outer core.

Meltwater Water that comes from melting snow or ice, including glaciers.

Moorland A habitat found in higher elevations, characterized by low vegetation such as shrubs.

Mountain range A group of mountains that form a line and are connected.

Plate boundary An area where two or more tectonic plates meet.

Plate tectonics The scientific theory that Earth's crust is made up of large, slow-moving plates.

Rainforest A forest found in the tropical or temperate zones that is characterized by high humidity and high rainfall.

Sediment Solid material left behind by water, wind, or ice.

Seismometer A tool that measures movements of the ground, like an earthquake.

Shield volcano A type of volcano made up of hardened lava that is low and wide.

Sonar A tool that uses sound waves to detect objects underwater.

Tectonic plate A massive slab of rock that floats on Earth's crust.

Tundra An area of land with no trees, not much vegetation, and a layer of soil that is always frozen—usually found in the Arctic regions or high on mountain tops.

Weathering A process caused by wind, water, and ice that wears away material such as rock and sediment.

Index

A
Abbott's duiker antelopes 25
Aboriginal peoples 30–31
Alps 10
Andes 4, 10
Appalachian Mountains 10, 11
ash 22, 23

B
bases, mountain 5
Basin and Range Province 16

C
Cascade Range 22
Chagga people 26–27
cinder cone volcanoes 23
climate 4
climate change, and glaciers 24, 36–37
composite volcanoes 22

D
deodar cedar 13

E
Earth, plate tectonics 6–7, 8, 10, 17, 33, 34
earthquakes 7, 35
economy 20
ecosystems, Mount Kilimanjaro 25
El Capitan 21
erosional mountains 9, 28–29
Uluru 30–31
experiments
    fossils 38–39
    model volcanoes 40–41

F
Fairview Mountain 9
farming 15, 27
fault-block mountains 8, 16–17
    Sierra Nevada 18–19
fold mountains 8, 10–11, 42
    Himalayas 12–13
fossil-making experiment 38–39
fuel 14, 15

G
General Sherman 21
giant lobelias 25
giant sequoias 18–19, 21
glaciers 24, 28, 36–37
great gray owls 19

H
Harz Mountains 17
Hawaiian Volcano Observatory (HVO) 34–35
Himalayan tahr 13
Himalayas 10, 12–13, 36
    life in the 14–15

I
Indigenous peoples 20, 26–27, 30–31

J
Jackson's chameleons 25

K
Kathmandu 14
Kibber Village 14
Kīlauea 34
Kilimanjaro National Park 26
Kings Canyon National Park 21
Kirkjufell Mountain 28

L
Lake Tahoe 20
lasers 35
lava 22, 23, 34–35

M
magma 8, 22, 24, 33
Marangu village 27
Mauna Kea 32
meltwater 36, 37
mid-ocean ridge 32–33
mountains, defined 4–5
Mount Elbert 8
Mount Fuji 8
Mount Hood 22
Mount Katahdin 28
Mount Kilimanjaro 24–25

life on 26–27
Mount Ngāuruhoe 41
Mount Rushmore 29
Mount Whitney 18

N
national parks 9, 18, 21, 26, 30
Nevada City 21

P
Parícutin 23
peaks 5
Piton de la Fournaise 23
plate tectonics and tectonic plates 6–7
   and fault-block mountains 16, 17
   and fold mountains 10, 11
   and Mount Kilimanjaro 24
   and underwater mountains 33
pyrometers 35

R
red kangaroos 31
red pandas 13
ridges 5
Rocky Mountains 8

S
sandstone 30
science
   monitoring volcanoes 34–35

mountain glaciers and climate change 36–37
seamounts 33
seismometers 35
Sequoia National Park 21
serval cats 25
shield volcanoes 23, 34
Sierra bighorn sheep 19
Sierra fence lizards 19
Sierra Nevada 18–19
   life in the 20–21
slopes 5
snow leopards 13
sonar 32
South America, Andes 4, 10
South Lake Tahoe 20
spectrometers 35
Steens Mountain 8
summits 5

T
Taconic Mountains 42
Tahoe yellow cress 19
Tanzania 24, 25, 26, 27
tectonic plates, see plate tectonics and tectonic plates
Teton Range 16
tourism 20, 26, 30
types of mountains, see erosional; fault-block; fold; volcanic

U
Uluru 30–31
underwater mountains 32–33

V
valleys 5
volcanic mountains/volcanoes 7, 8, 22–23, 34, 41
   model volcano experiment 40–41
   monitoring 34–5
   Mount Kilimanjaro 24–27

W
weather 4, 12, 36
weathering 28
World Glacier Monitoring Service 37

Y
yaks 14, 15
Yosemite National Park 9, 21

Acknowledgments

The publisher would like to thank the following for their kind permission to reproduce their photographs:

(Key: a-above; b-below/bottom; c-center; f-far; l-left; r-right; t-top)

123RF.com: Koba Samurkasov 34, 36; **Alamy Stock Photo:** Associated Press / U.S. Geological Survey 35tl, Jessica Ball / USGS 35bl, Ken Barber 8-9tc, Frank Bienewald 15t, Christoph Gerigk / Biosphoto 33br, blickwinkel / McPHOTO / BLE 31tl, Saraya Cortaville 15clb, Ulrich Doering 27tr, GeoJuice 37tl, Juergen Hasenkopf 27br, Bert Hoferichter 26bl, Hum Images 35tr, imageBROKER.com GmbH & Co. KG / uenter Fischer 37bl, David Litschel 20-21tc, José María Barres Manuel 25cr, Michael & Patricia Fogden / Minden Pictures 31clb, Ernst Mutchnick 19cr, Natural History Collection 19crb, Steven Noroian 42cra, Doug Perrine 33bc, Peter Schickert 31bl, Matthew Patrick / USGS 34b, Bianca Otero / ZUMA Press Wire 24tr; **Dreamstime.com:** 44Photography 17b, Galyna Andrushko 22crb, Bennymarty 30crb, Serhii Bezrukyi 25bl, S Billingham 19tr, Mariusz Blach 20b, Anastassiya Bornstein 21tr, Bryan Busovicki 34crb, Christiannafzger 20br, Maria Luisa Lopez Estivill 11tl, Fosna13 30b, Frhojdysz 33bl, Robert Van Gils 30cra, James Griffiths 28cra, Jianqing Gu 12l, Hel080808 31r, Hotshotsworldwide 19tl, Indiatraveler 14tr, Daniel Johansson 15b, Kathy25 11tr, Aleksandr Koltyrin 37tr, Ralf Lehmann 34tr, Saikit Leung 4cra, Lukich 22, Makasanaphoto 36b, Mikael Males 13tr, Matauw 11bl, Max5128 12-13b, William Attard Mccarthy 14b, Brandy Mcknight 25br, Phillip Minnis 31cla, Minnystock 21bl, Moizhusein 24br, Danilo Mongiello 27tl, Pranodh Mongkolthavorn 28b, Mopic 6cra, Nyker1 18, Grondin Franck Olivier 23b, Thomas Olson 16, Pancaketom 9br, Dmitry Pichugin / Dmitryp 41br, Daniel Prudek 37br, Adam Ramsey 29b, Joe Ravi 12-13tc, Rhallam 4, RightFramePhotoVideo 35br, Movado Salatoga 15cra, Shotsbykurt 13ca, SimonDannhauer 21br, Miroslaw Skorka 23t, SI Photography 5t, Srijun8 25tr, Srlee2 8-9bc, Dietmar Temps 24-25b, Thecriss 10b, Kelly Vandellen 9tr, Willeye 43, Wirestock 8bl, 19b, 26cr, Wiktor Wojtas 27bl, Dmitriy Yakovlev 17t; **NASA:** 11br; **Science Photo Library:** Library Of Congress 32bl

Cover images: *Front:* **Dreamstime.com:** Tomas1111 cr; **Shutterstock.com:** Graphic toons t, Vixit bl; *Back:* **Alamy Stock Photo:** Christoph Gerigk / Biosphoto bl; **Dreamstime.com:** Makasanaphoto tl, Joe Ravi cl